Book Five

Step by Step
Piano Course

by
Edna Mae Burnam

To my cousins

PLAYBACK+
Speed • Pitch • Balance • Loop

The exclusive *Playback+* feature allows tempo changes without altering the pitch.
Loop points can also be set for repetition of tricky measures.

To access audio, visit:
www.halleonard.com/mylibrary

Enter Code
6225-0646-4155-1625

ISBN 978-1-4234-3609-6

WILLIS MUSIC

T0057334

EXCLUSIVELY DISTRIBUTED BY

HAL•LEONARD®
7777 W. BLUEMOUND RD. P.O. BOX 13819 MILWAUKEE, WI 53213

Visit Hal Leonard Online at
www.halleonard.com

TO THE TEACHER

This is Book Five of EDNA MAE BURNAM'S PIANO COURSE — STEP BY STEP.
It is designed to follow her BOOK FOUR by presenting new subjects in logical order and, ONE AT A TIME.

Sufficient work is given on each step so that the student will thoroughly comprehend it before going on to the next step.

Besides the explanatory remarks and the music that the student will learn to comprehend and play, this book contains a musical dictionary of the words and musical signs used in this book.

When the student completes this book the following subjects will have been learned:—

    1. Learned to name and play the following **new** notes:—

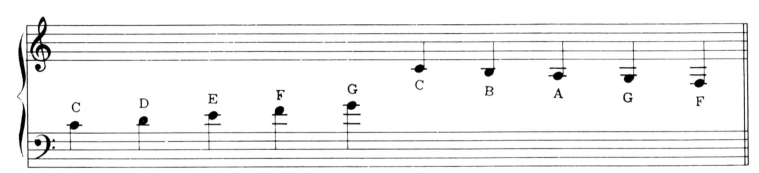

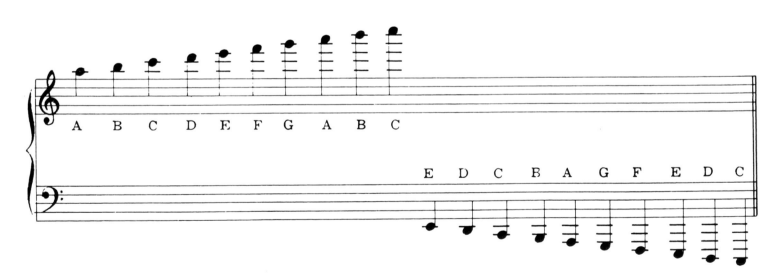

    2. Read and play in the following key signatures:—

C Major	E Major
G Major	F Major
D Major	B-Flat Major
A Major	E-Flat Major

3. The use of the damper pedal.

4. Understand the signs $8^{- - - - - - \urcorner}$ and $8_{\ldots\ldots\lrcorner}$

5. Play and count dotted quarter notes.

6. Read and play a piece for right hand only.

7. Read and play a piece for left hand only.

8. Play treble clef notes with the **left** hand.

9. Play bass clef notes with the **right** hand.

10. Count and play sixteenth notes.

11. Count and play pieces in $\begin{smallmatrix}6\\8\end{smallmatrix}$ meter.

12. Learned the meaning and pronunciation of the following new musical words:—

Alla marcia
Allegretto
Allegro
Andantino
Coda
Cantabile
Giocoso
Introduction
Maestoso

WHEN THE BAND GOES BY

Alla marcia means
in march time.

Alla marcia

USING THE PEDAL

When the pedal is used correctly, it can make music sound more beautiful. The pedal on the right (called the **damper** pedal) is the one you are going to use at present.

This pedal is used by the **right** foot. The **ball** of the foot should rest **on the pedal.** The **heel** of your **right** foot should be **on the floor** as you press the pedal down, and as you release the pedal.

Your heel acts as a **hinge**—as your foot presses down and lifts up.

Your teacher will show you how to sit comfortably and place your foot properly on the pedal.

Now—press the pedal down **gently**—then release it.

Keep your heel **on the floor.**

Practice this several times to get the "feel" of using the pedal.

THE PEDAL MARK

This is a pedal mark.

The line going **down** means to **press the pedal down.**   The pedal is **held down all through this line.**   The line going **up** means to **release the pedal.**

When a pedal mark begins **under** a note, the pedal is to be **pressed down immediately after the note is played.** The pedal must **catch the sound** of that note! And, it should be **kept down** through all of the notes above the line of that pedal mark. The pedal is **released where the pedal mark ends.**

Play the following examples using the pedal as marked.

TWO SHORT PEDAL MARKS

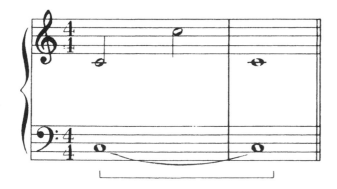
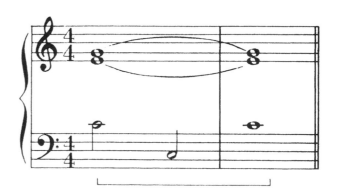

A LONGER PEDAL MARK

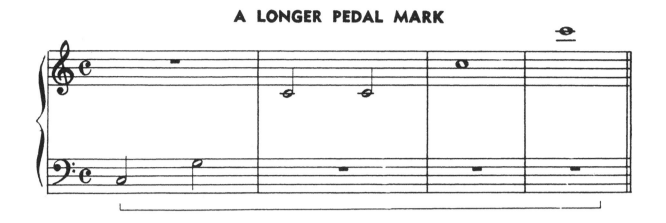

Pedal this piece correctly.

RAINBOW

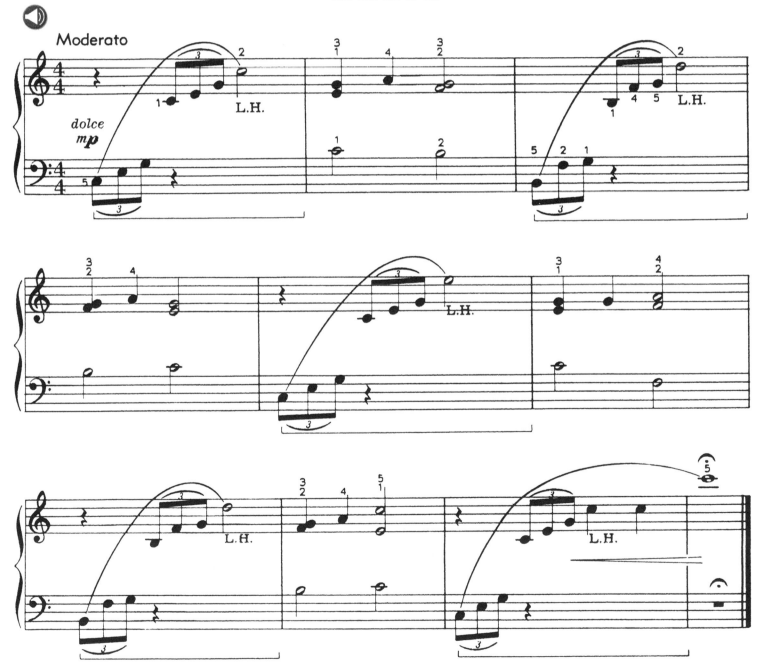

PEDALING FOR CONSECUTIVE MEASURES

Look at the pedal marks for the third and fourth measures of A DEEP CANYON. Each measure has a separate pedal mark! You must **release** the pedal as marked at the **end** of **measure three,** then **press** the pedal **down** on the **first count of measure four.**

A DEEP CANYON

A piece in the key of **B-Flat Major**—with pedal.

COLORED WINDOWS

LEGATO PEDALING

When you see a pedal mark like this ⌞ ⌃ ⌃ ⌟ it means you should make the **pedal-change** as **smoothly connected** as possible.

The pedal is **released** just as the new note is played—and is **pressed down again immediately.**

IN CHURCH

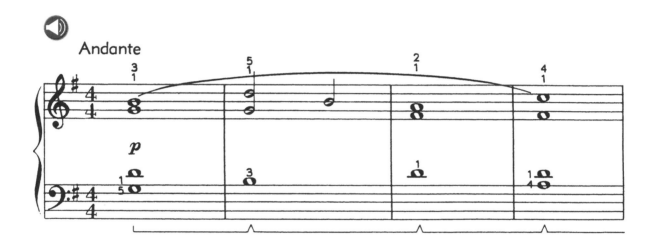

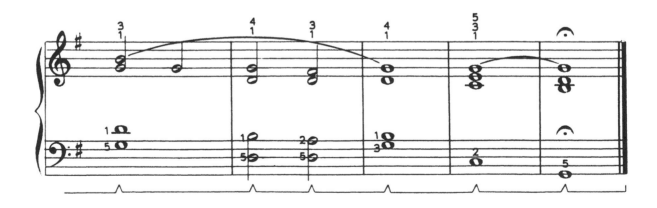

When there is a sign like this $8\text{------}\rfloor$ **below** a note, or chord, or group of notes it means these notes are to be played **one octave lower.**

MARCH OF THE FOOTBALL BAND

Marcato

When there is a sign like this $8\!-\!-\!-\!-\!-\!-\!\urcorner$ **above** a note, or chord, or group of notes it means these notes are to be played **one octave higher.**

SKYLINE OF A LARGE CITY

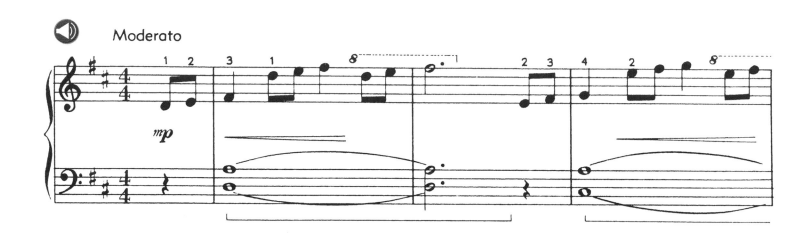

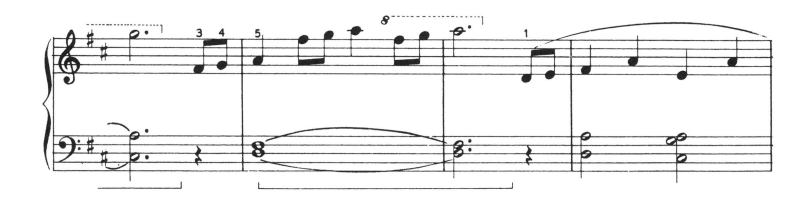

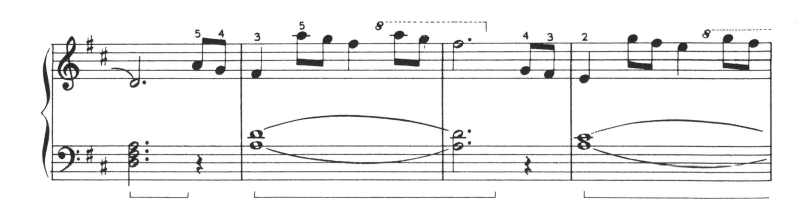

SOME NEW LEGER LINE NOTES

Usually notes **above** middle C are written in the treble staff like this

Sometimes it is necessary for the **left** hand to play these notes. When this happens they are written like this

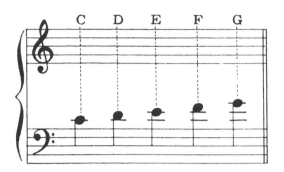

These leger line notes are easy to play and read if you **think** how **far away they are from MIDDLE C** as you play them.

C and **one note higher** to D

C and **skip up one note** to E

C and a **skip up, and one note higher** to F

C and a **skip up and and another skip up** to G

Remember—**these are the same notes**—only

The left hand plays these

The right hand plays these

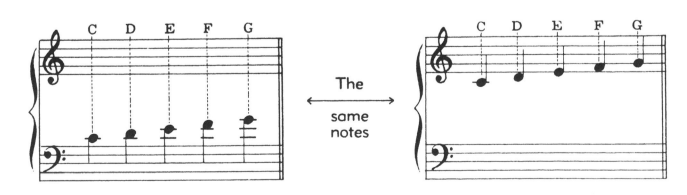

The ⟷ same notes

SCALE-LIKE RUNS

Every run in this piece has the same fingering as the C Major scale.

Allegro means fast.

FREEWAY TRAFFIC

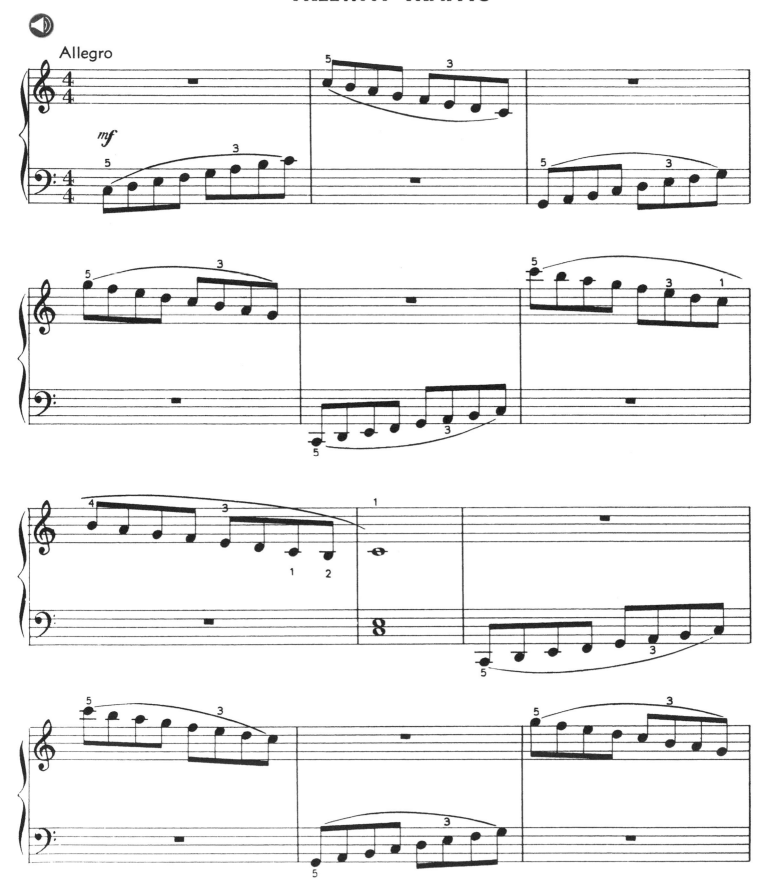

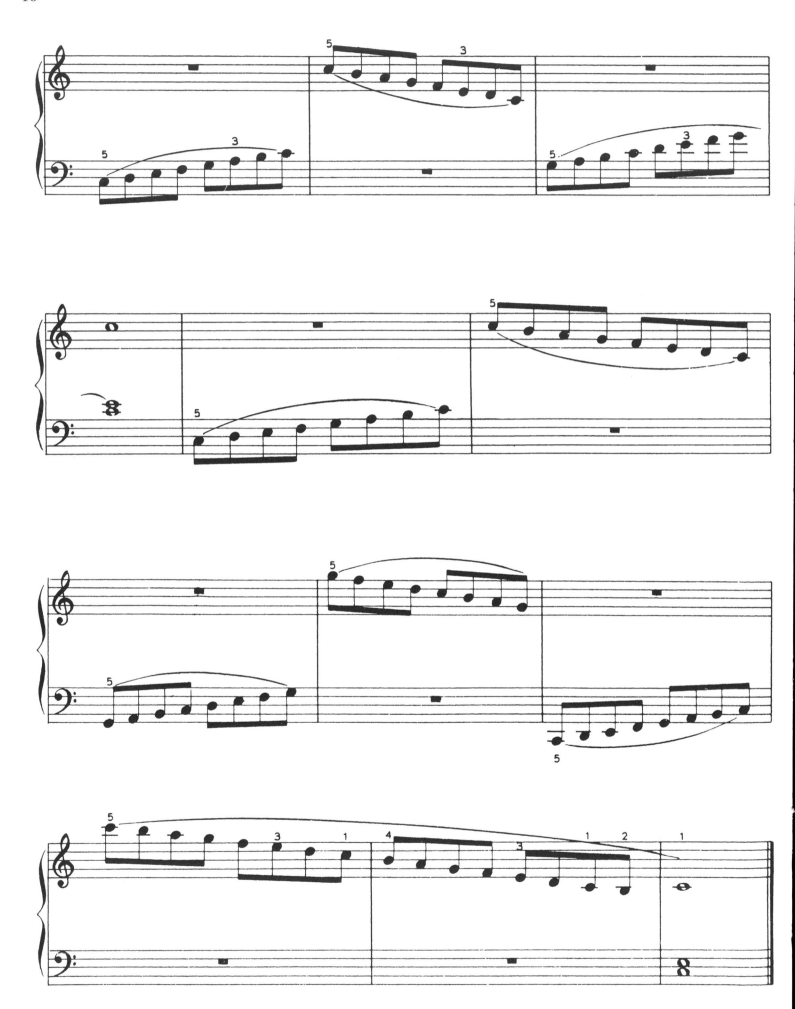

Allegretto means light and lively.

THE CLOCK ON THE WALL

KEY OF A MAJOR

Notice the key signature of this piece.

It is in the key of **A Major**.

Remember to sharp every F, C, and G as you play.

THERE ARE BLOSSOMS ON OUR CHERRY TREE

Giocoso means
with humor.

BIRDS IN THE BIRDBATH

DOTTED QUARTER NOTES

A **dot** placed **after** a note **adds** to that note **one half of its value.**

Here is a **dot** placed **after a quarter note.** ──────→

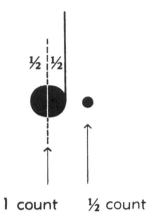

1 count   ½ count

You know that a quarter note gets **one count.** Half of this is only ½ count.

So the dot only gets ½ a count.

A dotted quarter note is usually followed by an eighth note to complete the unfinished count.

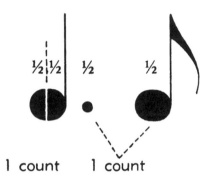

1 count   1 count

An easy way to count dotted quarter notes is like this

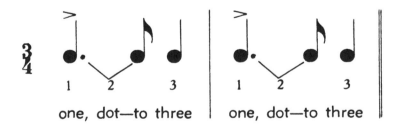

one, dot—to three | one, dot—to three

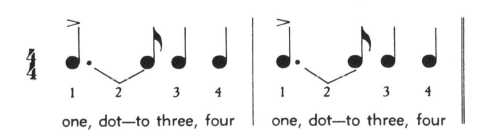

one, dot—to three, four | one, dot—to three, four

ROUND AND AROUND

Look at the third measure of this piece.

The dotted note comes on count three.

This is the way to count the first line of this piece:—

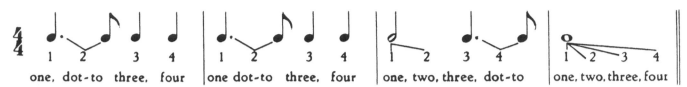

one, dot-to three, four | one dot-to three, four | one, two, three, dot-to | one, two, three, four

ALL THROUGH THE NIGHT

Andante

Arr. by E. M. Burnam

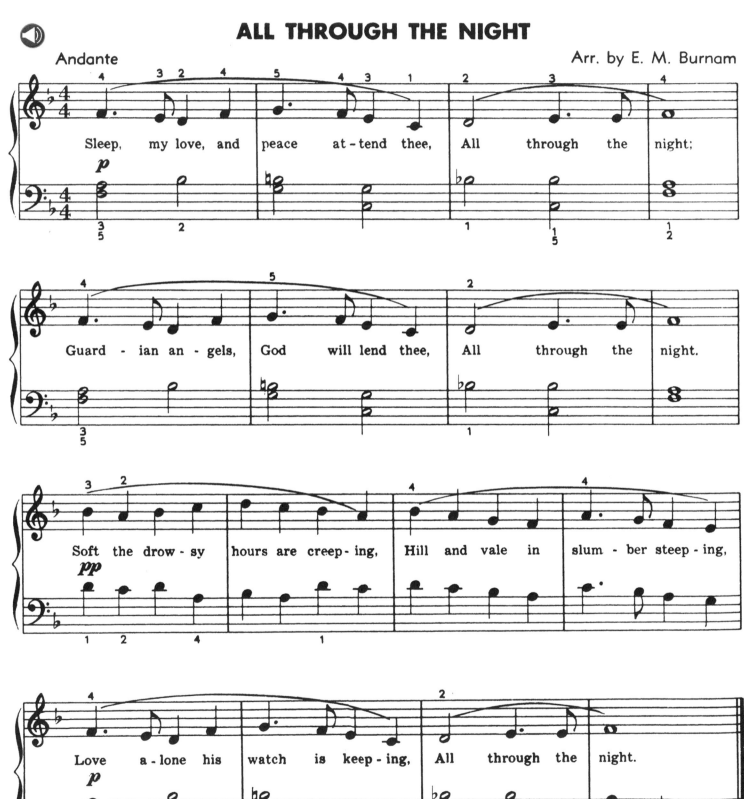

Sleep, my love, and peace at-tend thee, All through the night;

Guard - ian an - gels, God will lend thee, All through the night.

Soft the drow-sy hours are creep-ing, Hill and vale in slum - ber steep-ing,

Love a-lone his watch is keep-ing, All through the night.

SOME MORE LEGER LINE NOTES

Usually notes **below** middle C
are written in the bass staff like this

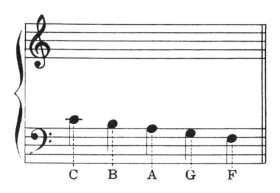

Sometimes it is necessary for the **right** hand to play these notes.

When this happens, they are written like this:—

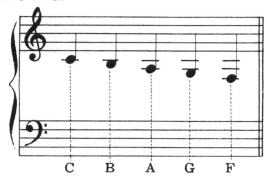

These leger line notes are easy to read and play if you **think** how **far away they are from MIDDLE C** as you play them.

C—then **one** note **lower** to B

C—then **skip down one** note to A

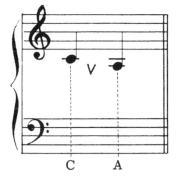

C—then **skip down and one note lower** to G

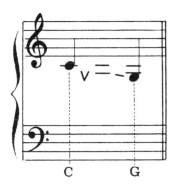

C—then **skip down and another skip down** to F

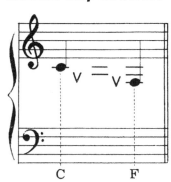

Remember—these are the same notes

only

The **left** hand plays these

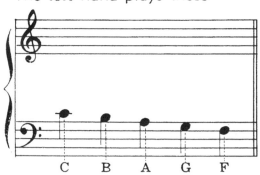

The **right** hand plays these

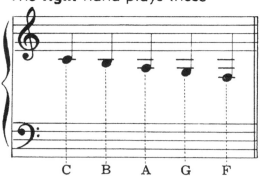

TWILIGHT THOUGHTS

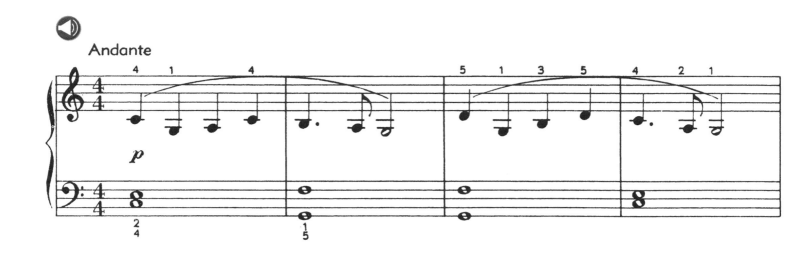

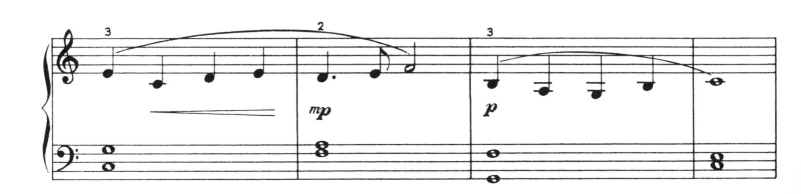

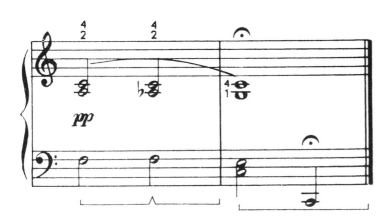

PIECE FOR RIGHT HAND ONLY

The left hand rests throughout this entire piece.

If you pedal correctly, the piece will sound as though two hands are playing it!

BROKEN ARM MELODY

A PIECE FOR LEFT HAND ONLY

The right hand rests throughout this entire piece.

Follow the dotted lines—and play the piece with your **left** hand.

Maestoso means in
a majestic style.

TO A SUBMARINE

Maestoso

THE LEFT HAND READS TREBLE CLEF

Up to this time the **right** hand has played notes written after the **treble clef,** and the **left** hand has played notes written after the **bass clef.**

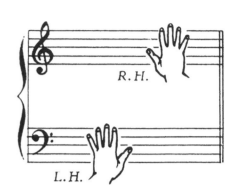

Sometimes the **left** hand has to play notes **above** MIDDLE C. When this happens, the **left hand part** may have a **treble clef sign.** When the **left hand notes** are written **after a treble clef sign,** they are read just the same as if they were written in the staff for the right hand.

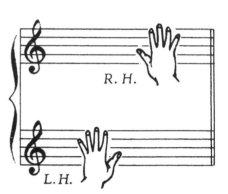

These notes are the same—only

The **left** hand plays these   The **right** hand plays these

The
same

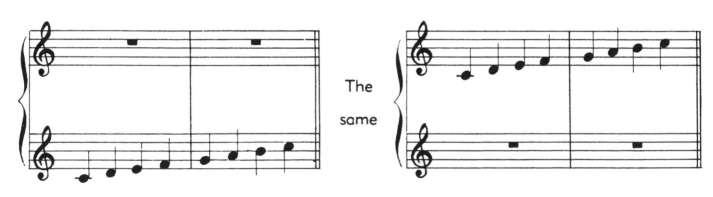

Now **both** hands read the treble clef.
Be sure to play the third and fourth measures correctly!

Watch the change of clef in the left hand part.

I HEAR AN ECHO

SUNRISE IN THE MORNING

OVER CANDY COTTON CLOUDS

INTRODUCTION—a section to prepare the ear for the actual piece.

CODA—an additional section to conclude a piece.

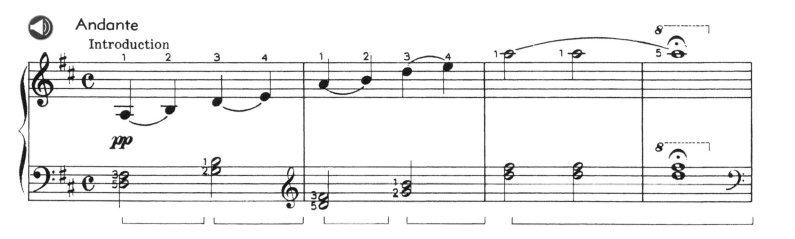

We flew up, up, up in the air, O-ver can-dy cot-ton

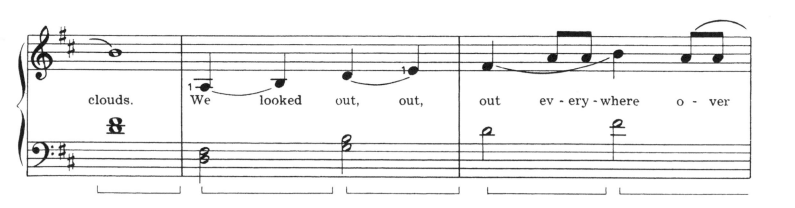

clouds. We looked out, out, out ev-ery-where o-ver

32

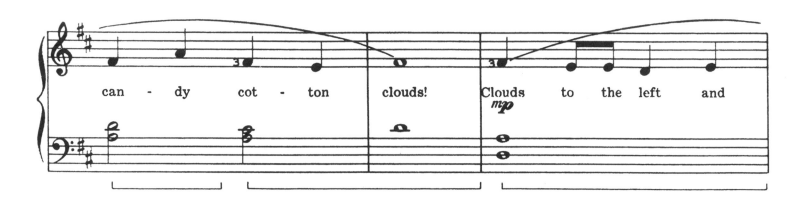

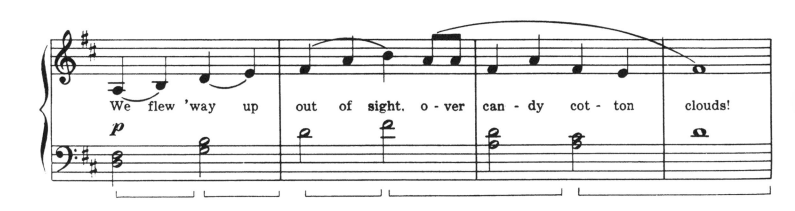

SOME NEW LEGER LINE NOTES

You know the first leger line note above the treble staff is A.

The other leger line notes are easy to read if you think how far they are from this A.

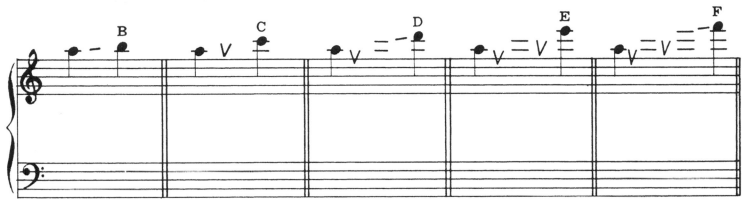

A—and one note higher to—B

A—and skip up a note to—C

A—skip up, and one note higher to—D

A—skip, and skip again to—E

A—skip, skip and one note higher to—F

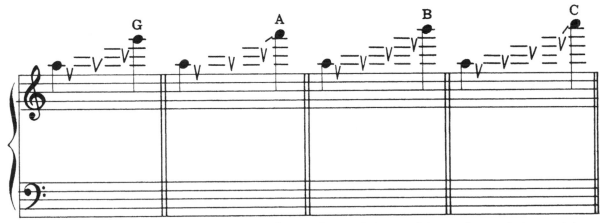

A—skip, skip, skip to—G

A—skip, skip, skip and one note higher to—A

A—skip, skip, skip, skip to—B

A—skip, skip, skip, skip and one note higher to—C

Here are all of these notes in order.

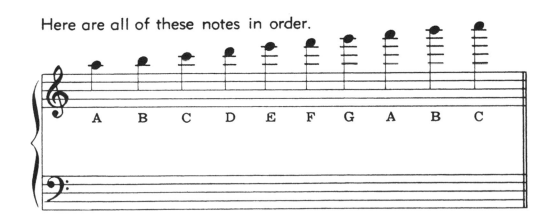

A B C D E F G A B C

Cantabile means
in a singing style.

OUR CHURCH HAS A STEEPLE TALL

HELICOPTERS

Allegretto

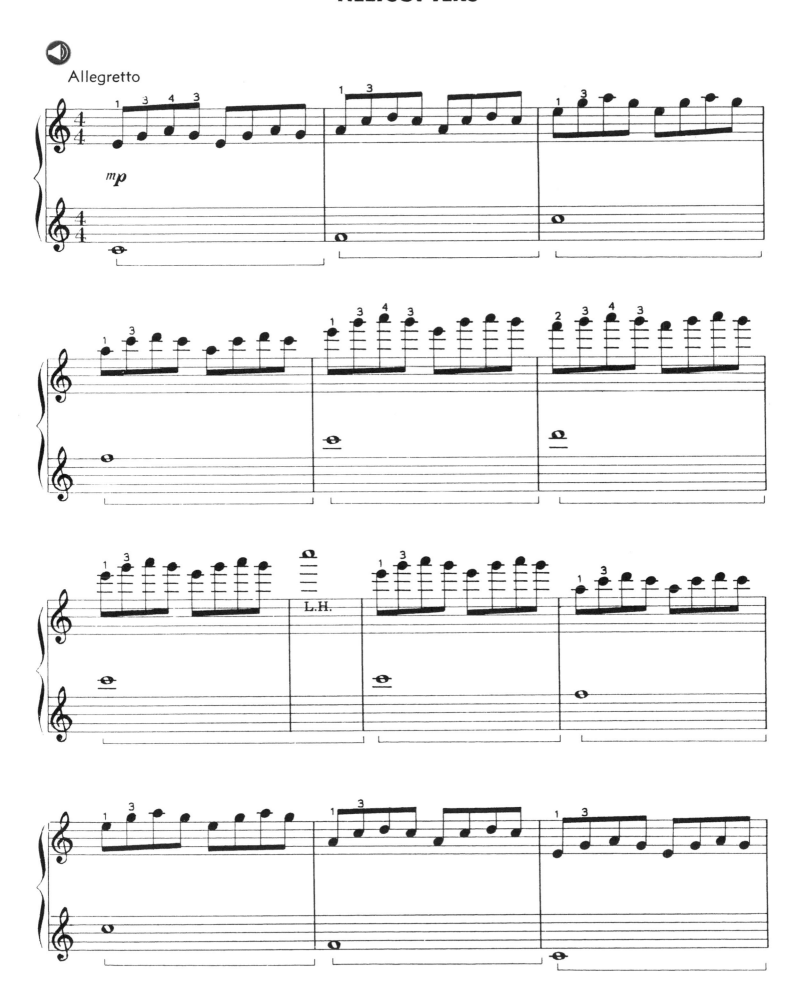

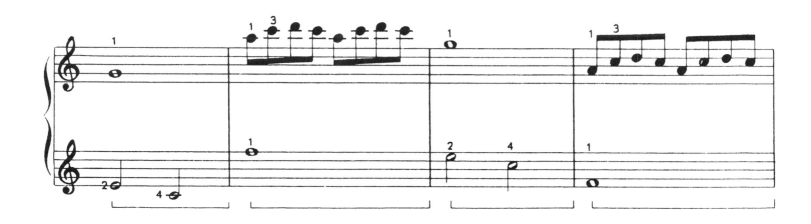

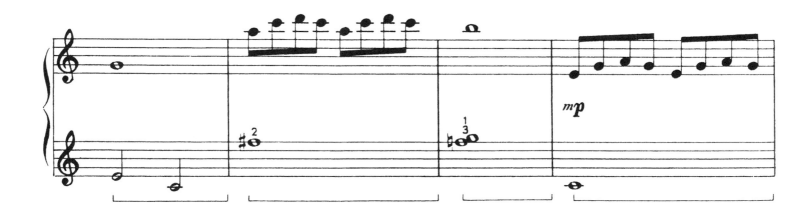

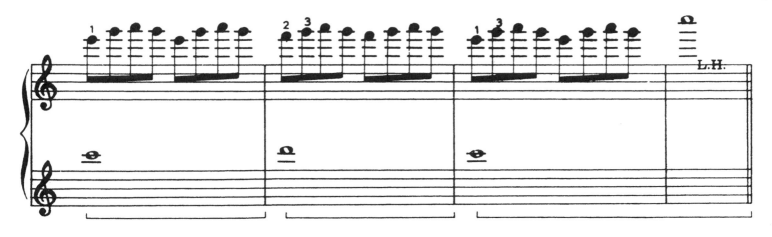

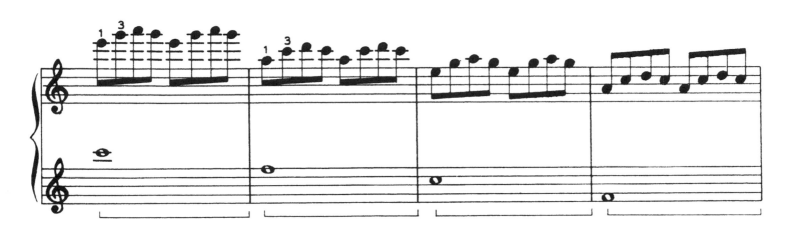

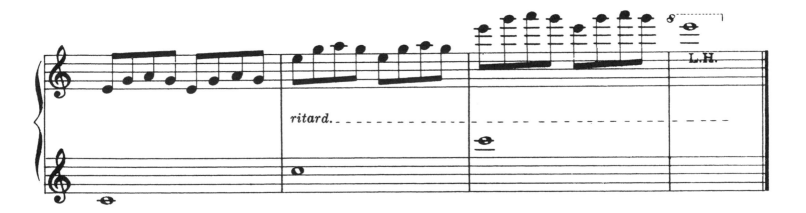

KEY OF E MAJOR

Notice the key signature of this piece.

This is the key of E major.

Remember to **sharp** every F, C, G, and D.

DAYDREAMS

SIXTEENTH NOTES

You know a **quarter** note gets **one** count. _____ ♩ = 1 count

You know that an **eighth** note gets **one half** a count. _____ ♪ = ½ count

You know that **two eighth** notes get **one** count. _____ ♫ = 1 count

Here is a **sixteenth** note. _____ ♬

A **sixteenth** note gets **one fourth** of a count. _____ ♬ = ¼ count

Four sixteenth notes get **one** count. _____ ♬♬ = 1 count

Two sixteenth notes get **one half** a count. _____ ♬ = ½ count

Here are these notes in order, according to their value.

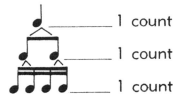

_____ 1 count

_____ 1 count

_____ 1 count

Play and count the following studies.

TUMBLING

Giocoso

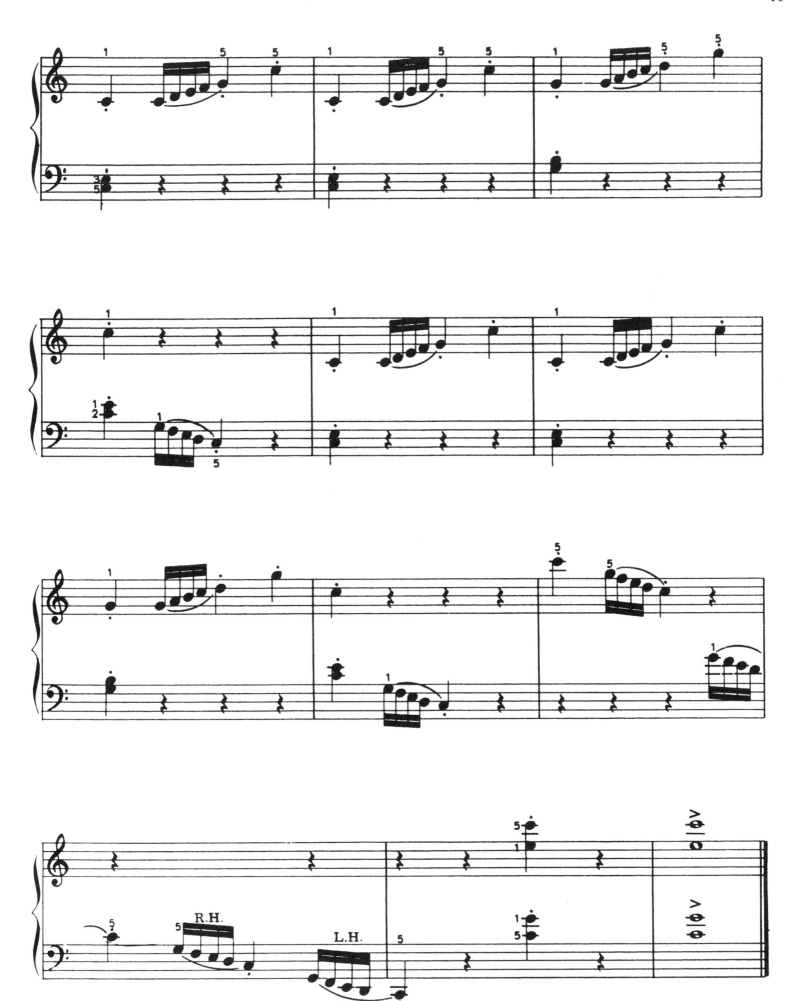

BASEBALL

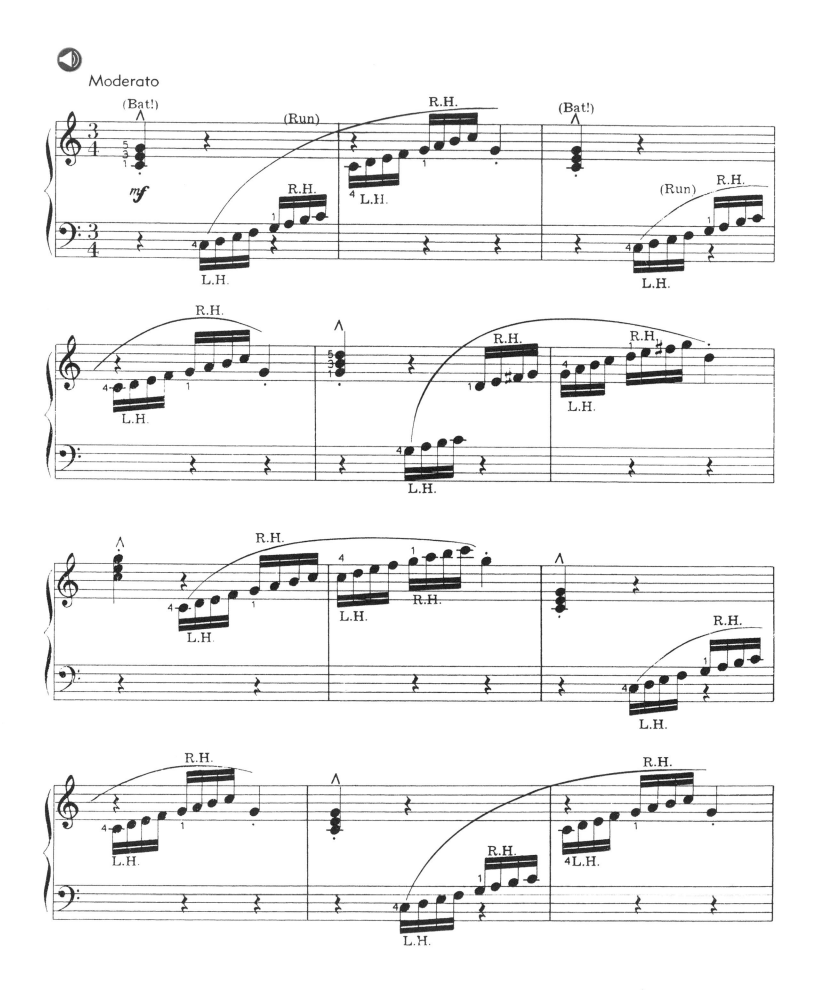

(wind-ups)

44

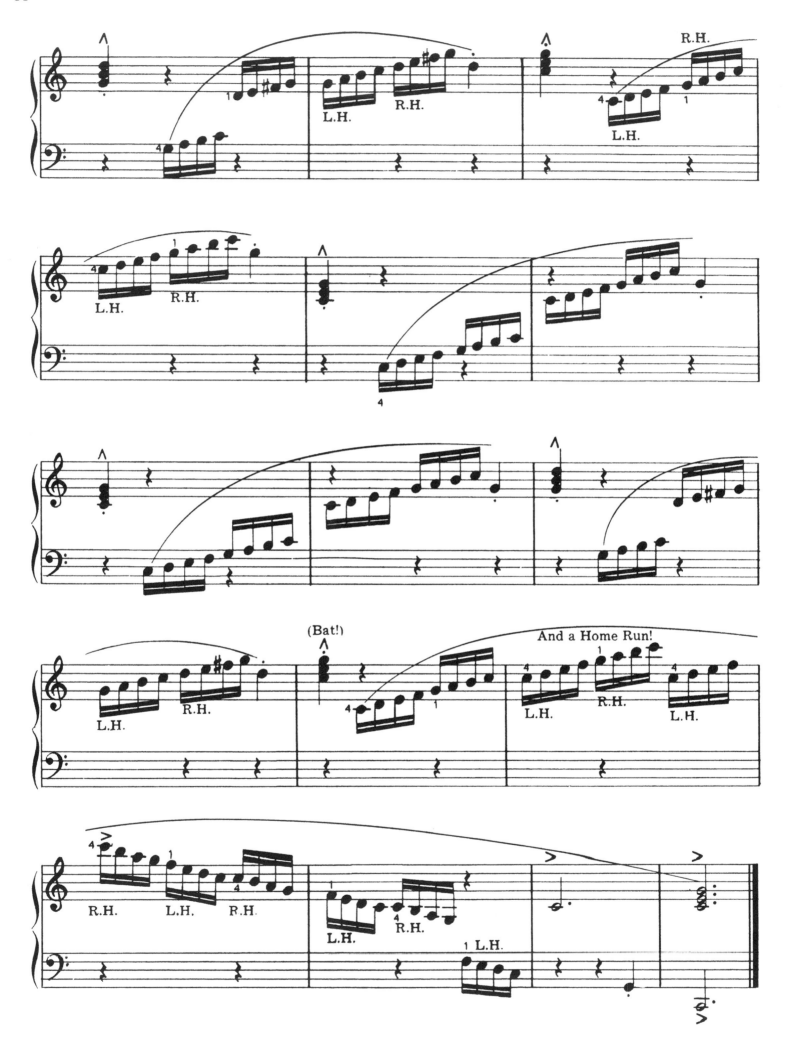

KEY OF E-FLAT MAJOR

Notice the key signature of this piece.

This is the key of **E-flat major**.

Remember to **flat** every B, E, and A.

WALTZ IN
E-FLAT MAJOR

THE RIGHT HAND READS THE BASS CLEF

Sometimes the **right** hand has to play notes written **below** middle C.

When this happens, the **right** hand part may have a **bass clef sign.**

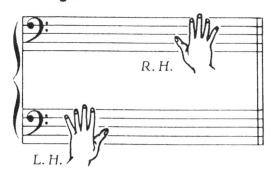

These notes are the same—only

The **left** hand plays these

The

same

The **right** hand plays these

Now **both** hands read the **bass** clef.

ON THE DEEP SEA

SOME NEW LEGER LINE NOTES

You know that the **first leger line note below** the bass staff is **E.**

The other leger line notes are easy to read if you think how far they are from this E.

E—and one note lower to—D E—and skip a note down to C E—and skip down, and one note lower to B E—and skip and skip again to A E—skip, skip, and one note lower to G

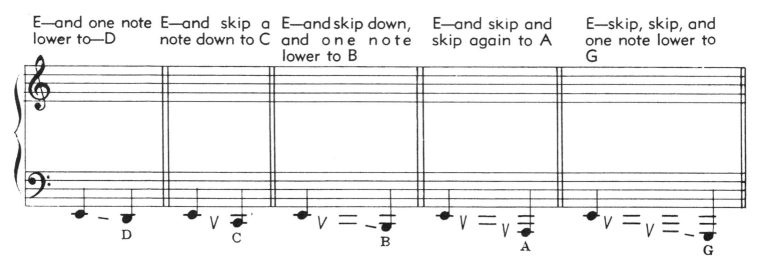

E—and skip, skip, skip to F E—and skip, skip, skip and one note down to E E—and skip, skip, skip, skip to D E—and skip, skip, skip, skip, and one note lower to C

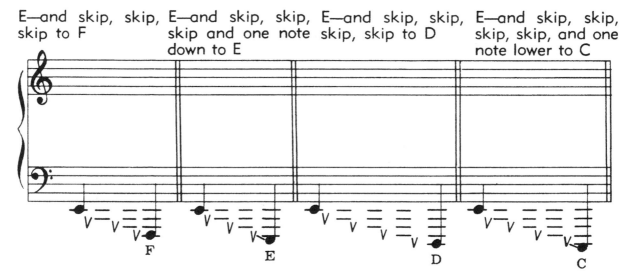

Here are all of these notes in order.

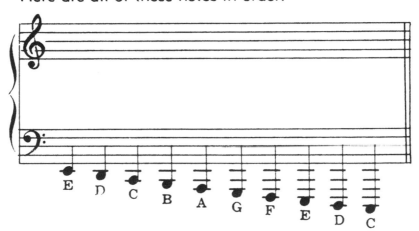

THE POOL IS DEEP

MARCH OF THE CLOWNS

(for left hand only)

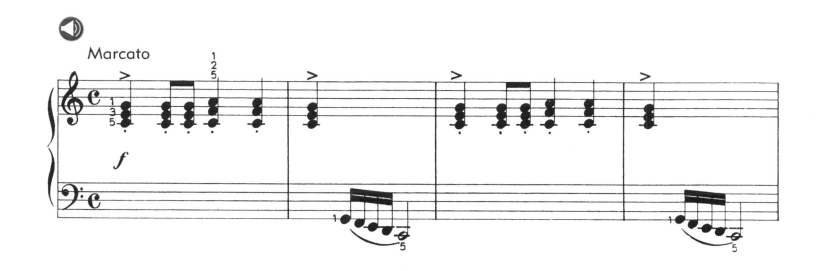

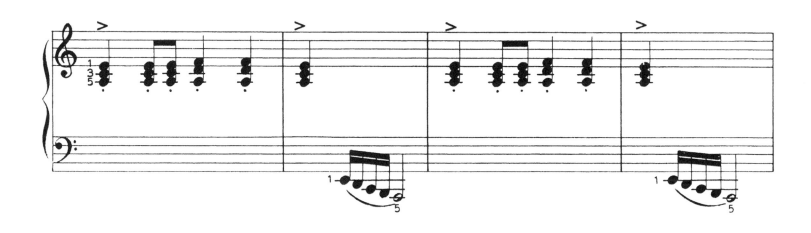

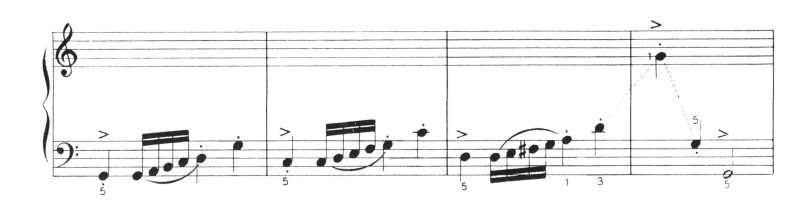

51

IN A GLASS BOTTOM BOAT

$\frac{6}{8}$ METER

Notice the time signature.

The **top** number tells how many **counts** there are in **each measure.**

There are **six counts** in **each measure.**

The **bottom number** tells **what kind of a note gets one count.**

An **eighth note** gets **one count.**

Count and play the exercise below.

Accent counts are **one** and **four.**

In $\frac{6}{8}$ meter a **quarter** note (♩) gets **two counts.**

Now count and play the next exercise.

In $\frac{6}{8}$ meter a **dotted quarter note** (𝅘𝅥𝅭) gets **three counts.**

Now count and play the next exercise.

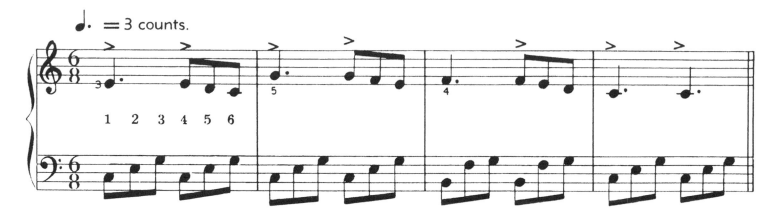

In $\frac{6}{8}$ meter a **dotted half note** (𝅗𝅥.) gets **six counts.**

Now count and play the next exercise.

In $\frac{6}{8}$ meter an **eighth rest** (𝄾) gets **one count.**

Now count and play the exercise below.

In $\frac{6}{8}$ meter a **quarter rest** (𝄽) gets **two counts.**

Now count and play the exercise below.

In $\frac{6}{8}$ meter every note or rest gets **twice as many counts** as it would in $\frac{4}{4}$ $\frac{3}{4}$ or $\frac{2}{4}$ meter.

In $\frac{4}{4}$ meter   In $\frac{6}{8}$ meter

In $\frac{4}{4}$ meter	In $\frac{6}{8}$ meter
♪ = ½ count.	♪ = 1 count.
♩ = 1 count.	♩ = 2 counts.
♩. = 1½ counts.	♩. = 3 counts.
𝅗𝅥 = 2 counts.	𝅗𝅥 = 4 counts.
𝅗𝅥. = 3 counts.	𝅗𝅥. = 6 counts.

Count and play the exercise below.
Accent counts are **one** and **four.**

REMEMBERING

Andantino

EVENING

FIREWORKS IN THE SKY

AMERICAN MARCH

Alla marcia

f

A - mer - i - ca, A-

mer - i - ca, My coun-try great and free. A - mer - i - ca, A - mer - i - ca, I

pledge my loy - al - ty. Our arm - y and our nav - y, too, Pro - tect us night and

day. They'll fight to keep our free -dom in the U. S. A.'

DICTIONARY OF MUSICAL TERMS
USED IN THIS BOOK

WORDS

Andante ....slow

Andantino ....slow—but not as slow as andante

Alla marcia..in march time

Allegro ....fast

Allegretto ....light and lively

Cantabile ....in a singing style

Coda ....an additional section to conclude piece

Crescendo ....gradually louder

Dolce ....softly and sweetly

Fine ....the end

Giocoso ....with humor

Introduction ....a section to prepare the ear for the actual piece

Maestoso ....in a majestic style

Moderato ....moderate speed

SIGNS

D. C. al Fine— return to the beginning and play to **Fine**

mp — mezzo piano—moderately soft

p — piano—soft

pp — pianissimo—very soft

mf — mezzo forte—moderately loud

f — forte—loud

ff — fortissimo—very loud

$>$ — accent

⌢ — pause

⌐_____⌐ — pedal

⌐___∧___⌐ — pedal

◁_____ — gradually louder

▷_____ — gradually softer

$\mathbf{C}$ — $\frac{4}{4}$ meter

8^{------} — play an octave higher

8_{------} — play an octave lower

Certificate of Merit

This certifies that

....

has successfully completed

BOOK FIVE
OF
EDNA MAE BURNAM'S
PIANO COURSE

STEP BY STEP

and is eligible for promotion to

BOOK SIX

....Teacher

Date...

Edna Mae Burnam was a pioneer in piano publishing. The creator of the iconic *A Dozen a Day* technique series and *Step by Step* method was born on September 15, 1907 in Sacramento, California. She began lessons with her mother, a piano teacher who drove a horse and buggy daily through the Sutter Buttes mountain range to reach her students. In college Burnam decided that she too enjoyed teaching young children, and majored in elementary education at California State University (then Chico State College) with a minor in music. She spent several years teaching kindergarten in public schools before starting her own piano studio and raising daughters Pat and Peggy. She delighted in composing for her students, and took theory and harmony lessons from her husband David (a music professor and conductor of the Sacramento Symphony in the 1940s).

Burnam began submitting original pieces to publishers in the mid-1930s, and was thrilled when one of them, "The Clock That Stopped," was accepted, even though her remuneration was a mere $20. Undaunted, the industrious composer sent in the first *A Dozen a Day* manuscript to her Willis editor in 1950, complete with stick-figure sketches for each exercise. Her editor loved the simple genius of the playful artwork resembling a musical technique, and so did students and teachers: the book rapidly blossomed into a series of seven and continues to sell millions of copies. In 1959, the first book in the *Step by Step* series was published, with hundreds of individual songs and pieces along the way, often identified by whimsical titles in Burnam's trademark style.

The immense popularity of her books solidified Edna Mae Burnam's place and reputation in music publishing history, yet throughout her lifetime she remained humble and effervescent. "I always left our conversations feeling upbeat and happy," says Kevin Cranley, Willis president. "She could charm the legs off a piano bench," Bob Sylva of the *Sacramento Bee* wrote, "make a melody out of a soap bubble, and a song out of a moon beam."

Burnam died in 2007, a few months shy of her 100th birthday. "Music enriches anybody's life, even if you don't turn out to be musical," she said once in an interview. "I can't imagine being in a house without a piano."